The NAVAJOS
People of the Southwest

NANCY BONVILLAIN

NATIVE AMERICANS
THE MILLBROOK PRESS
BROOKFIELD, CONNECTICUT

Cover photograph courtesy of the Wheelwright Museum of the American Indian

Photographs courtesy of Photo Researchers: pp. 8 (© Sylvain Grandadam), 50 (© George Chan), 53 (© Porterfield/Chickering); National Archives: p. 11; Superstock: pp. 15, 22; American Museum of Natural History: pp. 19 (neg. no. 316436), 20 (neg. no. 14473), 31 (trans. no. 4128), 33 (bottom, trans no. K4417); Amon Carter Museum, Fort Worth, Tex.: p. 24 (Laura Gilpin Collection 7995/90); Museum of Northern Arizona: p. 27; Stephen Jett: p. 39 (top); Bettmann: p. 39 (bottom), 44, 47; Museum of New Mexico: p. 42. Map by Joe LeMonnier

Library of Congress Cataloging-in-Publication Data
Bonvillain, Nancy.
The Navajos : people of the Southwest / by Nancy Bonvillain.
p.   cm. — (Native Americans)
Includes bibliographical references and index.
Summary: the history and culture of the Navajos, the largest Native American tribe in the United States today. The story of the Navajos is brought up to the present in this volume, and traditional songs and recipes are included.
ISBN 1-56294-495-9
1. Navajo Indians — Juvenile literature.   [1. Navajo Indians. 2. Indians of North America — Southwest, New.]   I. Title.   II. Series.
E99.N3B59 1995   979′.004972 — dc20   94-21818   CIP   AC

Published by The Millbrook Press, Inc.
2 Old New Milford Road, Brookfield, Connecticut 06804

CONTENTS

The Navajos

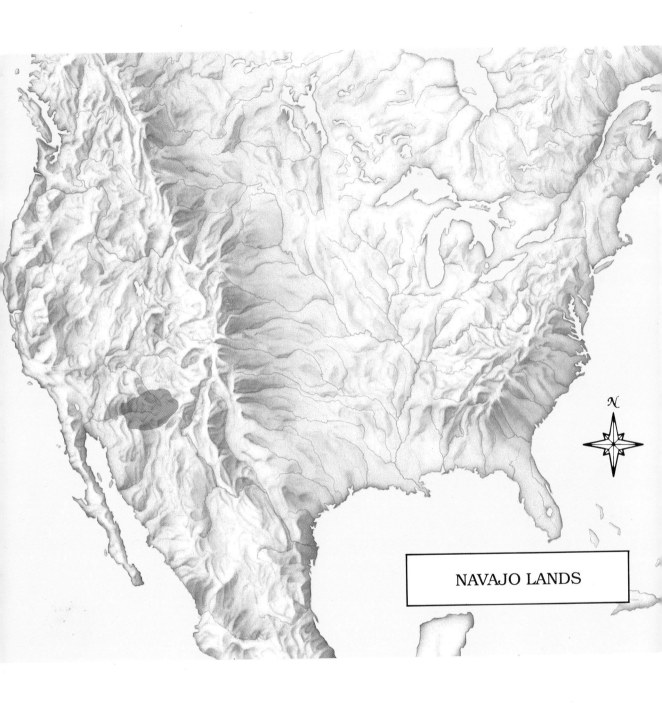

NAVAJO LANDS

FACTS ABOUT
THE TRADITIONAL NAVAJO
WAY OF LIFE

GROUP NAME

Navajo; Diné ("the people")

GEOGRAPHIC REGION

Southwest: Arizona, New Mexico, Utah

LANGUAGE

Athapaskan

HOUSE TYPE

Six- or eight-sided house, called a "hogan,"
made of logs, brush, and mud

MAIN FOODS

Corn, beans, squash, wild plants, deer, rabbits

In the 1800s the Canyon de Chelly, with its strange and dramatic rock formations, was home to hundreds of Navajos living in northeastern Arizona.

Chapter One

THE LONG WALK

The year was 1863. In June the United States Army launched a war against the Navajos. The United States had just won the Mexican-American War and taken possession of the Southwest. Now the U.S. government wanted to control Native Americans living in New Mexico and Arizona. Although government authorities had succeeded in forcing many native groups to submit to their power, the Navajos resisted. The government responded by calling out its army.

While army officers were planning the war, General James Carleton asked Navajo leaders to come to a meeting in the town of Santa Fe, New Mexico. There Carleton told the Navajos that the United States government wanted them to leave their homeland and surrender at Fort Sumner in eastern New Mexico. The general warned the leaders that if they did not go to Fort Sumner, he would send troops against them. The Navajos refused Carleton's orders. They had always been independent and would not give up their freedom voluntarily.

General Carleton then put Colonel Christopher (Kit) Carson in charge of the war. Carson was told to round up the

Navajos and bring them to Fort Sumner (also called Bosque Redondo). Carson's troops were joined by New Mexican settlers and by Utes, Native Americans who were enemies of the Navajos. New Mexicans and Utes planned to capture Navajo women and children to sell as slaves to American settlers.

Carson began an invasion of Navajo territory. He ordered his soldiers to destroy cornfields and peach trees planted by the Navajos. The soldiers also killed the Navajos' horses and sheep, burned down their homes, and ruined their water holes. By destroying the people's food and shelter, Carson hoped to make them surrender. Some Navajos did give up because they were starving, but many others escaped and hid in the deep canyons and remote hills of their vast homeland.

In the first six months of Carson's campaign, soldiers killed 301 Navajo men, women, and children. Eighty-seven others were wounded and 703 were captured. New Mexican settlers and Utes killed or captured hundreds more.

In the early months of 1864, Carson attacked Navajos living in the Canyon de Chelly (pronounced "shay") in northeastern Arizona. Two hundred people surrendered, thirty-four were captured, and many others were killed. The survivors were forced to march on what came to be called the "Long Walk" to Fort Sumner, a distance of more than 300 miles (483 kilometers). In the cold of winter, without enough food or warm clothing, many Navajos starved or froze to death along the way. Soldiers shot sick or weak people who could not keep up with the march. Pregnant women who stopped to give birth were also killed.

During the course of the year, the army captured thousands of Navajos. Thousands more surrendered, hoping at least to save their lives. By March 1865, a total of 9,022 Navajos were imprisoned at Fort Sumner. No one knows how many people avoided capture or death by hiding, but at least several thousand remained free.

The Navajos were shocked by the actions of the United States Army. They wondered why the U.S. government had waged a war against them. What had the people done to deserve such a fate?

The Navajos called their years of imprisonment at Fort Sumner nabondzod — *"the fearing time." By the time this photograph was taken in 1866 at Fort Sumner, the Navajos had been kept at the fort in a state of near-starvation for two years.*

THE NAVAJOS UNDER SIEGE ■ Trouble between the Navajos and the government began in 1848 when the war between Mexico and the United States ended. The government wanted to subdue the Indians in the Southwest so that American settlers could move into the region. Settlers complained that Navajos raided their farms, taking crops and horses. The settlers did not admit that they attacked the Navajos, trying to force them out of their own homes and land or capture them to sell into slavery.

Navajo leaders met with government officials several times in the late 1840s. The officials demanded that the Navajos stop their raids, but did not offer to protect the Navajo people from the settlers' attacks. Sometimes tensions flared at the meetings. At one session in 1849, a Navajo leader named Narbona refused to make one of his aides give up a horse that a Mexican soldier said belonged to him. As the Navajos left the meeting, Narbona and six of his followers were murdered, shot in the back by soldiers.

In 1851 the United States Army built a fort, called Fort Defiance, in the middle of Navajo territory. The army hoped that the presence of soldiers nearby would frighten the Navajos. Despite the threat posed by the soldiers, the Navajos defended themselves and their land.

A few years later, U.S. officials convinced a number of Navajo leaders to sign a treaty. By the terms of the Bonneville Treaty of 1858, the Navajos agreed to give up some of their territory. More American settlers and ranchers then moved to Navajo lands. As tensions increased, the Navajos realized that the U.S. government would never protect them from settlers coming to their territory.

Three years later, the Navajos and the government signed another treaty, pledging to live in peace. The treaty acknowledged that New Mexican slave traders had captured many Navajos. But although the government promised to defend the people, it did nothing to stop the raids. In fact, soldiers attacked Navajos who retaliated against the settlers.

Government officials decided that the only way to make the region safe for settlers was to defeat the Navajos once and for all. Governor Henry Connelly of New Mexico then named General Carleton to plan the war.

After the Long Walk to Fort Sumner in 1864, the Navajos faced many hardships. New Mexicans continued to capture Navajos to sell as slaves even while the people were held near the fort. Living conditions at Fort Sumner were inhumane. Families lived in holes dug in the ground, covered only with cowhides and brush. The Navajos suffered from malnutrition and disease because the army did not give them enough food or clean drinking water. As a result, two thousand people died.

After four years of imprisonment, the Navajos were released. A new treaty was signed between the Navajos and the United States government in which the two groups promised to live in peace. However, the government would not let the Navajos keep all of their former territory. The Treaty of 1868 set aside a reservation for the Navajos along the Arizona–New Mexico border that was only one tenth the size of their lands. But the Navajo leaders accepted the terms because the people wanted to be free.

The Navajos left Fort Sumner in June 1868 in a column that stretched for 10 miles (16 kilometers). Thus began their second Long Walk. This time, the people were glad because they were returning home. Although the Navajos' imprisonment ended, their descendants today still tell the story of that tragic period of Navajo history.

NAVAJO ANCESTORS ▪ Ancestors of the Navajos came into what is now the southwestern United States after a long journey from western Canada. They probably left Canada about one thousand years ago. It took many generations to reach the Navajos' present-day location. They arrived sometime in the eleventh century.

As they traveled south along the Rocky Mountains and western plains, they hunted animals in the woods and prairies, caught fish in the rivers, and gathered wild plants, roots, berries, and nuts. By the time they reached the Southwest, they were separated into two groups. One group became known as the Navajos and the other as the Apaches. The languages of the Navajos and Apaches belong to a linguistic family called Athapaskan. Other Athapaskan languages are spoken by native people in western Canada, all of whom are distant relatives of the Navajos.

In their own language, the Navajos call themselves *Diné* (pronounced dee-NAY), a word meaning "the people." And they call their original homeland in the Southwest *Dinetah*. Dinetah was located in northwestern New Mexico and northeastern Arizona, south of the San Juan River in a wide, fertile valley. The name Navajo means "planted fields in a valley." The name was applied to the Diné by the Spanish in the seventeenth century. It is not a Spanish word, but rather comes from a native New Mexican language called *Tewa*.

Some early dwellings of the Puebloans still survive today, nestled against the protective walls of the Canyon de Chelly.

When ancestors of the Navajos arrived in the Southwest, they met other Native American peoples living nearby. These groups had cultures that were very different from that of the Navajos, who were hunters and gatherers. Their new neighbors were farmers, growing crops such as corn, beans, and squash. These peoples are now known collectively as Puebloans, from the Spanish word *pueblo*, meaning "people."

Ancestors of the Navajos learned farming skills during or soon after their journey to the Southwest. Some may have learned to farm from Native Americans in the Plains, while others borrowed agricultural methods from Puebloans in the Southwest. By the sixteenth century, the Navajos had taken up farming, but they still hunted deer, rabbits, mountain sheep, and other animals. They gathered wild plants and nuts to add to their diet.

The Navajos lived peacefully with most of their neighbors in the Southwest. They traded with the Puebloans, giving them deer meat, deerskins, and salt. In return, the Navajos received cotton cloth.

Life in Dinetah began to change in the late sixteenth century when Spanish soldiers and settlers invaded the region. The Spanish came into the Southwest from Mexico, where they had conquered the Aztecs. They tried to force the Puebloans, Navajos, and Apaches into submission. Spanish soldiers defeated many Puebloans, but they never conquered the Navajos.

Through the centuries since Europeans arrived in North America, the Navajos saw their region controlled by three foreign governments. First came the Spaniards, then the Mexicans, and finally the American settlers. Even though there have been many changes in the lives of the Diné, the people have kept their own language and cultural traditions. They follow their unique practices and beliefs. And Navajo leaders today are a strong voice speaking for their people.

Chapter Two

COMMUNITY LIFE

The Navajo Nation contains nearly 15 million acres (6.8 million hectares) of land located in the four neighboring states of New Mexico, Arizona, Utah, and Colorado. Its territory includes plains, foothills, mountains, and mesas. The Navajo Nation has some of the most beautiful and majestic landscapes in the United States.

The land of the Navajo Nation is high above sea level, ranging from 3,500 to 10,000 feet (1,067 to 3,048 meters). Yearly rainfall is low, with averages of 5 to 11 inches (12.7 to 28 centimeters) per year. Most of the rain comes in sudden and severe storms in the summertime. But the strong sun, dry air, and high winds cause moisture to evaporate quickly.

The land itself is dry. Only a few rivers run through the Nation. Navajos depend on small streams and springs for their supplies of water.

TRADITIONAL NAVAJO COMMUNITIES ▪ Navajos traditionally lived in small settlements consisting of a group of families related on the mother's side. A group that lived in the same settlement might contain an older couple, their daughters and daughters' families, and their unmarried sons.

Usually each family consisting of a mother, father, and children had its own home in the settlement. The homes were built close to one another and formed a unified group. When a woman married, she usually stayed with her mother's group. Her husband left his own kinspeople and moved into his wife's settlement.

A traditional Navajo house, called a *hogan*, was built with a distinctive design. It was six- or eight-sided in shape, with a rounded roof. Hogans were made from logs, brush, and mud. The door of a hogan always faced east, the direction of the rising sun.

In addition to its hogans, each settlement group had land that it used for farming and grazing animals. Land was not owned by individuals but rather was controlled for use by the group as a whole.

In traditional Navajo settlements, the eldest woman was recognized as the head of the group. She managed the group's affairs and saw that all necessary work was done. She had influence because of her wisdom and experience. When important matters were discussed or decided, people also asked for advice from their mother's brothers and sisters.

NAVAJOS' DAILY WORK ▪ All people living in a household and settlement shared the work that needed to be done. Some tasks usually were done by women, others by men, but most were performed by both women and men.

Family life took place both within and outside the many-sided hogans of the traditional Navajo settlement.

Women took care of the household, including cooking meals and cleaning the home. Child care was also mainly a woman's responsibility. And in addition, many women were weavers. They set up looms, spun wool into yarn, colored the yarn with various vegetable and mineral dyes, and wove blankets and rugs with geometric designs. Navajo weavers made blankets and rugs for their family's use and for sale outside their territory.

Navajo women's skill at weaving provided their families with items for their own use as well as income from sales to people outside their settlements.

Navajo Fried Bread

This fried bread can be topped with tomatoes, onions, cheddar cheese, lettuce, and pinto beans to make a traditional taco.

Ingredients
> 4 cups flour
> 1 tablespoon baking powder
> 1 teaspoon salt
> 2 tablespoons powdered milk
> 1½ cups warm water
> 1 cup lard or shortening

Preparation
1. Put the flour in a bowl, add the baking powder, salt, and powdered milk. Mix together.
2. Mix in the warm water to form dough.
3. Knead dough by hand until it is soft but not sticky. Cover with a cloth and allow to stand for about 15 minutes.
4. Shape dough into balls about 2 inches (5 centimeters) across, then flatten by patting and stretching the dough with hands and fingers until the dough is flat and round (or roll it out using a rolling pin).
5. Melt the lard or shortening about an inch deep in the frying pan. The fat should be hot before the dough is put in. Fry one side, then turn and fry the other until both sides are golden brown.

The vast and sandy valleys of Navajo territory have always been more suitable for the raising of sheep and goats than for the cultivation of crops.

Men cleared the land for farming and built the hogans. They also hunted animals such as deer, prairie dogs, rabbits, and mountain sheep.

Men did most of the farmwork. The Navajos' main crop was corn. Other crops included beans, squash, and fruits. Navajo farmers used rainfall to water their crops. Only a few areas of their territory contained rivers or streams. In these places, men dug ditches from the rivers into their fields to water the crops.

Elsewhere, farming was difficult because of the low amount of rainfall. In addition, the timing of rain was crucial to farming. If summer storms came too early in the growing season, young plants might drown or wash away. If rain came too late, plants withered and died from lack of water.

Navajo women and men cared for their herds of animals. Herds consisted mainly of sheep and a few goats. The people valued sheep for their meat and wool. In addition, Navajos owned horses that they used for transportation. Some people also had cattle. Navajos rarely slaughtered cattle for food. Instead, they kept them for the cash they would bring when sold.

Everyone, including children above the age of about five years, owned some sheep and other animals. All the people in one settlement combined their animals into one herd. Men, women, and children helped take the herd to grazing land.

Members of a settlement often shared their food and shared the money brought in by sales of sheep and wool. They cooperated in farming and grazing animals. And they helped each other with daily tasks and in times of special need.

FAMILIES ▪ Although the kind of work most Navajos did in the past has changed over the years, family relationships remain the same today. Bonds between relatives were strong. The Navajos believed that kinspeople should be kind, helpful, and cooperative. These principles were important for all relatives. They were especially strong in the behavior of a mother and her children.

Mothers and children were linked together in a large social grouping called a clan. A clan was a group of people who consid-

A Navajo mother holds her child and two baby lambs. The woman's blouse is typical of early twentieth-century Navajo dress, with silver ornaments and decorative stitching.

ered themselves related to a common ancestor. Since a clan might contain thousands of people, individuals could not trace their actual relationship to all members of the clan, but they believed they were related. Each clan was named, most with the name of a place where the people believed their original clan ancestors had lived.

Since Navajo clans traced relationships through women, a child automatically belonged to the clan of its mother. Since clan members were relatives, people could not marry someone of their own clan. Therefore, a child's father always belonged to a different clan.

NAVAJO VALUES ▪ The Navajos believed that all living things had the right to live, to eat, and to act for themselves. All people were treated as equals. Women and men had equal rights and equal standing in their communities. Children, too, had individual rights that were not violated by adults. No one had the right to control anyone else, to force someone to do something, or to speak for another person.

Navajo values of individual rights meant that a group could not take actions unless the members all agreed. Decisions could be reached because the Navajos also believed that people should cooperate and understand the needs and wishes of others. The Navajos combined the two ideals of individual liberty and communal responsibility so that they could live together in harmony.

Chapter Three

THE NAVAJOS AND THE "HOLY PEOPLE"

Like all religions, the Navajo religion contains beliefs about the origin of the world and about the natural and supernatural beings that exist in the world. Like all believers, the Navajos perform ceremonies to honor the spirit beings.

THE NAVAJO UNIVERSE ▪ According to the spiritual beliefs of the Navajos, the universe consisted of a number of worlds, each in the shape of a round disk. The worlds, or disks, were stacked on top of each other, connected by colored columns.

Life began in the first, or bottom, world. In the beginning, the world was beautiful. People lived in peace and happiness. However, various disasters and misfortunes occurred as a result of quarrels and jealousies. The people then escaped to the next world, where life also began happily. But, as before, conflict and misery arose, causing the people to flee again to the next world. After a long time, the people finally emerged into the fifth, or current, world.

At the edges of the fifth world were four sacred mountains. (These mountains are identified today as Mount Taylor, Sierra

Blanca Peak, San Francisco Mountain, and Hesperus Peak.) The edges of the world were protected by four supernatural beings. Each being lay on the horizon between the cardinal directions of east, south, west, and north. Dawn Man lay on the horizon from east to south. Horizontal Blue Man lay from south to west. From west to north was Evening Twilight Woman. And Darkness Woman lay on the horizon from north to east.

This painting by a contemporary Navajo artist shows one of the four sacred mountains as described in the Navajo creation story. The male and female figures are sprinkling pollen on the eggs at the top of the mountain, which is decorated with white shells and corn and fastened to the earth by bolts of lightning.

HOLY PEOPLE ▪ The Navajos' universe was guarded by many deities, called Holy People. Holy People had the power to affect the lives of humans. They might use their powers to protect people, or they might punish wrongdoers.

Among the most important of Holy People were First Man and First Woman. They created the world by making a miniature version of it during an all-night ceremony. At sunrise, the miniature model was changed into the world as we have come to know it.

Another major deity was named Changing Woman. When Changing Woman grew to adulthood, she mated with Sun and had twin boys, called Monster Slayer and Born for Water. The twins then rid the world of monsters and other evil creatures. In doing so, they helped prepare the world for the emergence of the Navajos.

Changing Woman gave many gifts to the Navajos. She gave them corn, the food that became the people's central crop. And she created four pairs of people who started the four original clans. Because she created the clans and gave people their most valued food, Navajos often call her "mother."

Other deities were associated with animals, plants, and natural forms such as mountains, rivers, the moon, sun, and stars. Some Holy People were linked to natural forces including wind, rain, thunder, and lightning.

Deities had many of the same qualities as humans. They had the same bodily form and could think and speak like people. But, of course, they had much greater powers. And they had far superior knowledge.

A Modern Navajo Song

This song was written by
Arliene Nofchissey, a young Navajo
composer, songwriter, and actress.

The beat of my heart is kept alive in
*   my drum*
And my plight echoes in the canyons,
*   the meadows, the plains,*
And my laughter runs free with the deer,
And my tears fall with the rain,
But my soul knows no pain.

I am one with nature
Mother Earth is at my feet
And my God is up above me
And I'll sing the song, the song of
*   my people . . .*

NAVAJO CEREMONIES ▪ The Navajos performed a large number of ceremonies to please the Holy People and to protect humans from harm, and many of these ceremonies continue today. Although each ceremony had its own specific purpose, there were common themes that united them. Perhaps the basic theme of Navajo ritual was to maintain or restore beauty or harmony. The meaning of the Navajos' word for beauty was much more complex than the English word. In the Navajo language, beauty included all that was good, favorable, desirable, beautiful, pleasant, peaceful, and harmonious. The word referred both to these qualities and to the conditions in which they existed.

Ceremonies aimed to restore a proper balance between the good and evil that existed in the world. Navajos have never believed that people can eliminate evil entirely, but that it must be controlled so that beauty or goodness can prevail.

Ceremonies took place inside a hogan. They began at sunset and lasted from two to nine days. (The Navajos counted days from sunset until the next sunset, not from sunrise to sunrise.)

The Navajos conducted a number of different kinds of ceremonies or "sings." Each contained hundreds of prayers and songs performed by chanters, or singers. One ceremony was called Blessingway. Blessingway rites obtained the good powers of Holy People. They began with prayers that attracted the deities. The Navajos also made offerings of cornmeal and corn pollen to the Holy People. Corn and corn pollen were sacred substances, first given to the Navajos by Changing Woman. When a ceremony ended, Holy People judged whether it had been done properly. If so, Holy People gave good luck,

Masks worn during traditional Navajo ceremonies such as the Blessingway and Holyway rituals.

happiness, health, and long life to the human participants. Since Blessingway rituals brought beauty and goodness, the Navajos often included a Blessingway prayer at the end of other types of rituals to correct any mistake or omission that might have been made.

Another ceremony was called Holyway. Holyway ceremonies counteracted harmful forces. The Navajos believed that when people failed to maintain beauty and harmony, evil forces could get out of control. These forces then caused many kinds of misfortunes, including disease. Holyway rites therefore were often performed to treat illness.

The Navajos, like many peoples throughout the world, had a complex theory of the causes and treatments of illness. They believed that most ailments had a spiritual cause. When people got sick, they might consult a specialist who would diagnose the underlying reason for the ailment. The specialist, or "diagnostician," observed the patient and talked about his or her recent activities. A diagnostician might also perform rituals to find the reason for the illness. Once the cause was determined, a particular ceremony aimed at eliminating that cause would be recommended. The patient would then go to a chanter, or singer, who would perform the healing ritual.

The Navajos believed that a common cause of illness was contact with a harmful object or force. Various animals, insects, and plants were considered harmful. These included snakes, bears, porcupines, coyotes, ants, moths, and cactus. Natural forces such as whirlwinds, thunder, and lightning were also dangerous. Each of these dangers could be counteracted or eliminated by a specific Holyway ceremony.

During a curing ceremony or sing, the chanter took objects out of a sacred medicine bundle that had strong spiritual powers. The bundle might include gourds, rattles, painted sticks, feather wands, small pieces of turquoise and crystals, cornmeal, corn pollen, and herbal medicines. The chanter took each of these objects in turn and touched them to the patient. In doing so, healing powers contained in the objects were transferred to the patient.

Many Holyway rites included a dry painting (often called a sandpainting) made by the chanter and the chanter's assistants. A sandpainting was a representation of Holy People. It

*The finishing touches are put on a
sandpainting. This one is surrounded
by "feathers" of colored sand.*

was made on the floor of a hogan with sand colored with different pigments. Paintings varied in size. Most were about 6 feet (1.8 meters) in diameter, although some were as large as 20 feet (6 meters). It could take from three to five hours for the chanter to complete a painting.

When the sandpainting was finished, the patient sat on a portion of it. The chanter moistened his or her palms with herbal medicines, touched the painting so that sand stuck, and then applied the sacred sand to the patient's body. These actions transferred the healing powers of Holy People to the patient. The chanter next tied a jeweled bead into the patient's hair as a sign of a link to the Holy People. A female patient received a shell bead, while a male was given a bead of turquoise. These beads protected the wearer from harm.

During the last night of a Holyway cure, the chanter recited prayers and songs to end the ritual. The songs brought the good powers of Holy People and helped drive away the evil cause of illness. Then, as the sun began to rise, the patient left the hogan, faced east, and deeply breathed in the dawn air. The chanter offered a final prayer and repeated a Blessingway song.

■ ■ ■

Holyway and Blessingway rituals were effective because they helped people understand and cope with the problems they faced. These ceremonies are still performed today by the Navajos, to provide sacred links between the humans and the Holy People.

Chapter Four

FACING THE INTRUDERS

By the sixteenth century, the Navajos had established a secure way of life in the Southwest. They supported themselves by farming, hunting, and gathering wild plants. Their lives began to change in the later years of the century when invaders from Spain entered the region. From that time on, Navajos had to cope with increasing numbers of foreign intruders.

THE NAVAJOS AND THE SPANISH ▪ Spanish soldiers and settlers entered the Southwest from their base in Mexico. The Spaniards hoped to find rich treasures of gold and silver like those they had taken from the Aztecs in Mexico. Although the Spaniards did not find riches in the Southwest, they stayed in the area and waged wars to conquer the Puebloans living in small villages along the Rio Grande river.

As the Spanish advanced farther into the Southwest, they explored territory where the Navajos lived. According to Spanish reports of the period, the Navajos were the largest native group in the region. They were skilled farmers and hunters. Navajo men were also expert warriors.

The first meeting between the Navajos and Spaniards was friendly. In 1582 a Spanish official named Antonio de Espejo met a group of Navajos who gave him corn cakes as a gift of friendship. But the Spanish did not respond in kind. A few years later, Spanish soldiers attacked Navajo settlements. They killed many people and burned their cornfields.

As a result of the Spaniards' actions, the Navajos turned hostile toward the intruders. Relations between the Navajos and Spanish remained hostile throughout most of the seventeenth century. Spanish soldiers and settlers continually raided Navajo settlements, capturing people to sell as slaves to mining companies in central Mexico. The Navajos responded by defending themselves and attacking the Spanish.

The two groups had made several attempts to establish peaceful relations in the early years of the seventeenth century. During periods of peace, the Navajos traded with the Spanish. They gave the Spaniards corn, deer meat, and deerskins and in return received iron goods such as knives, nails, and axes. In addition, the Navajos obtained horses through Spanish trade. Although both groups benefited from the trade, the truce between them did not last long. Conflicts occurred with greater frequency by the middle of the century.

In 1680, Puebloans who were under Spanish control rose up in a united revolt against the Spaniards. They killed Spanish soldiers and priests living in their villages. This "Pueblo Revolt" forced the intruders out of the region. Only twelve years later, the Spanish again set out to conquer the Puebloans. Hundreds of Puebloans were killed in the bloodshed. By 1696, most Puebloan villages were again under Spanish control. During the reconquest, the Navajos helped the Puebloans by warning them of the Spaniards' advances and by raiding Spanish soldiers on the march.

Some Puebloan survivors of the massacres fled from their villages and took refuge among the Navajos. Most of the refugees were members of groups known as the Tewas and Hopis. Over time, the Puebloans intermarried with the Navajos and adopted Navajo culture.

SEARCH FOR A NEW HOMELAND ▪ Conflicts between the Navajos and the Spanish continued into the early eighteenth century. Although peace was established in the 1720s, the Navajos soon faced another enemy. The Utes began to raid Navajo settlements. As a result of nearly constant raiding, the Navajos left their homeland by 1754. They traveled south and west and reestablished their communities.

The Navajos were also pushed westward by Hispanic settlers from New Mexico who intruded on the eastern portion of their territory. In the 1770s the Navajos carried out several raids against settlers who were taking over their land. Although they drove out most of the settlers, many Navajos moved west where they hoped to find lasting security.

Conditions for the Navajos worsened in the early nineteenth century. Fighting again broke out between the Navajos and the settlers. In 1805, Spanish soldiers invaded the area surrounding Canyon de Chelly in northeastern Arizona, killing 118 Navajo men, women, and children.

When Mexico won its independence from Spain in 1821, the territories of New Mexico and Arizona came under Mexican control. Although the Mexican government promised to protect native inhabitants in the region, they failed to live up to their words. To make matters worse, Hispanic settlers got guns from U.S. traders who were entering the Southwest. They used the guns to attack Navajo communities to take captives for the slave trade.

SMALLPOX AND MEASLES ▪ In addition to deaths among the Navajos from centuries of armed conflict, thousands of people died from diseases brought into the region by the European and American settlers. The germs that caused smallpox and measles did not exist in North America before the arrival of Europeans. Since Native American people had never had these diseases, they did not develop any natural resistance or immunities to them. When European carriers of smallpox and measles came to North America, the diseases struck native communities with sudden and deadly force.

Throughout North America, millions of native people died. The Navajos suffered in large numbers. Between the middle of the sixteenth century and the middle of the seventeenth century, their population declined from at least ten thousand to only three or four thousand. But the Navajos made a remarkable recovery. By the early nineteenth century their population was again increasing, and today the Navajos number at least 160,000.

BROKEN PROMISES ▪ War broke out between the United States and Mexico in 1846, and two years later the United States took possession of the territories of New Mexico and

A rock painting by a nineteenth-century Navajo artist. The Spanish — dressed in long capes and broad-brimmed hats and carrying guns — are shown arriving on horseback to attack the Navajos. These paintings have been found throughout the Canyon de Chelly.

The war between Mexico and the United States was fierce and bloody. When the United States won and took over the territories of New Mexico and Arizona, the government failed to protect Navajos living in the region — despite a treaty with the Indians.

Arizona. The government wanted to make peace with the native people in the region. They signed a treaty with the Navajos in which both groups pledged to live in peace. Despite the words of friendship, government officials did nothing to stop New Mexican settlers from raiding the Navajos. Instead of protecting the Indians, the U.S. Army attacked Navajos who retaliated against the settlers. As tensions increased in the 1850s and early 1860s, the government began its campaign of war against the Navajos to subdue and imprison the entire population. That campaign ended in the "Long Walk" to Fort Sumner.

During four years of confinement at Fort Sumner, the Navajos suffered many hardships. When they were released in 1868, they returned to a land that had been destroyed by the soldiers. Their cornfields were burned, and their herds of sheep had been killed. But although conditions were bleak, the people resolved to rebuild their settlements and regain their good fortune.

Chapter Five

REBUILDING
THE HOMELAND

Before the Navajos were released from Fort Sumner, their leaders signed a treaty with the United States government. In the treaty, the government pledged to aid the people when they returned to their homeland. But the Navajos' territory was greatly reduced in size. It consisted of barely 3.5 million acres (1.4 million hectares), only about one tenth of their previous area. The territory no longer included most of the rich land that the people had used for farming and grazing.

By the terms of the treaty, the government promised to give food rations and other goods to Navajos for a period of ten years. However, the value of the rations was small, amounting to only about twelve dollars per year for each person.

RETURNING HOME ▪ Although the Navajos agreed to give up most of their territory, they kept the right to use their former lands if they were unoccupied. When the people returned home in 1868, most of these lands were not occupied by anyone else, but in a short time a growing number of American farmers and ranchers intruded into the region. In the 1860s there were

*A Navajo woman and her husband selling woven
blankets at a trading post in Arizona in 1885.*

approximately 100,000 settlers in New Mexico and Arizona. By
1890, there were almost 250,000. At the same time, the Navajo
population was also increasing. By the end of the nineteenth
century, they had nearly doubled their number to 20,000.

As the population of Navajos and settlers rose, the two
groups competed over a limited amount of land. Since the U.S.

government realized that the Navajos needed more land, their territory was enlarged through several presidential orders. Despite the increases, competition continued. Settlers intruded on more Navajo lands and harassed the people living there.

Even though conditions were often difficult, the Navajos enjoyed prosperity. Their herds of sheep grew rapidly. The people sold the sheep's wool to traders nearby. After 1882, when the Santa Fe Railroad laid tracks near their territory, Navajo women sold their woolen blankets and rugs to traders who shipped the products throughout the United States. In addition, tourists began visiting the Southwest. They bought Navajo rugs in large numbers. And Navajo silversmiths sold silver and turquoise jewelry to tourists and traders.

As the Navajos earned more money for their products, they bought more goods from traders, including foods, tools, utensils, and clothing. But in the last years of the nineteenth century, prices for wool and livestock fell. The people then had to rely on their own farming, herding, and hunting to survive.

THE GOVERNMENT STEPS IN ▪ In the late 1800s the U.S. government tried to manage Navajo life in several ways. First, the government opened boarding schools for Navajo children. American officials hoped that if children were separated from their families, they would accept American customs and values and then abandon their own traditions. Many Navajo parents refused to send their children to school because they did not want their children taken away from them. By the end of the nineteenth century, fewer than one hundred Navajo children attended school.

Most Navajo parents easily resisted the idea of sending their children off to the government-run boarding schools set up in the late 1800s. Not only were the children needed in the fields, but also the Navajos placed great value in having their children with them.

Second, the American government encouraged Christian ministers to go to Navajo territory to convert the people to Christianity. However, most Navajos continued to follow their own religious beliefs and practices.

In 1921, oil was discovered in the Navajo Nation. American oil companies wanted control of the rich oil and gas fields in the

Nation. However, they could not obtain leases because the Navajos had no centralized governing body that could approve contracts. American officials then stepped in and organized a Tribal Council, appointing twelve members. The Tribal Council immediately gave the United States Commissioner of the Navajo Tribe the power to sign oil and gas leases on behalf of the Navajos. But the Navajos were not paid fairly for their resources.

The Tribal Council gradually took greater responsibility for managing the Navajos' own government. They set up a police force and a system of courts. And they made decisions concerning the use of the vast amounts of money received from oil and gas companies operating in the Navajo Nation.

THE STOCK REDUCTION PROGRAM ▪ Although the Navajo economy was hurt by the Great Depression in the early 1930s, the people survived because they farmed their land and had large herds of sheep to supply them with wool and meat. Then, in 1933, their fragile stability was shaken by a new government policy. The policy, called stock reduction, was designed to deal with problems of severe soil erosion in the Nation caused by overgrazing. The Navajos were urged to sell a percentage of their sheep at fixed prices.

The Navajos strongly objected to this plan for several reasons. First, what the Navajos needed was more land and more water—not fewer sheep. Second, the government prices being offered for the sheep were very low. And third, the Navajos knew that once they sold their sheep, they would lose the yearly income they depended on from sale of the sheeps' wool.

Because of these objections, Collier's program failed in its early years; the Navajos simply refused to sell their sheep. Then, in 1936, the government divided the Navajo Nation into districts, each of which was allowed a maximum number of sheep. Any sheep over the limit had to be sold.

Government officials thought that the stock reduction program was a success because the total number of sheep owned by the Navajos was cut by more than half. However, to the Navajos stock reduction was a disaster. People resented the fact that their way of life was being controlled.

ADJUSTING TO CHANGE ▪ Since the Navajos lost much of their herds, many families could not support themselves from sales of wool and sheep. A majority of people had no other way to earn a living because there were very few job opportunities in or near the Navajo Nation. Some men had jobs building and repairing railroads, schools, and government offices. A number of women and men were migrant farmworkers in Colorado, California, and Idaho. But most people had no jobs. And those who did find work usually received very low wages.

The Tribal Council realized the hardships faced by many Navajos. In the 1940s and 1950s they set up several small businesses that gave jobs to local people. However, most of the businesses failed because they lacked funds. The Tribal Council then used some of its money from oil and gas leases to give financial aid to needy people.

Members of the United States Congress also realized that the Navajos were living in difficult conditions. In 1950 they passed the Navajo-Hopi Rehabilitation Act, which gave the Navajos and the neighboring Hopis a total of almost $90 million for

In one large, octagonal room, children in the first through fourth grades work together with a non-Indian teacher in a Navajo school typical of the 1950s.

improvements in their territories. The money paid for construction of wells, roads, schools, and health clinics.

By the middle of the twentieth century, the Navajos had adjusted to changes in their way of life. But even as conditions changed, the people were determined not to abandon their own traditions.

Chapter Six

THE NAVAJO
NATION TODAY

The Navajo Nation is home to about 160,000 people. They are the most numerous of all Native Americans. Throughout their history, the Navajos have faced many hardships, but they have survived with great strength and courage. Today the people assert their rights to control their own lives and lands.

The Navajo Tribal Council is the governing body of the Nation. The council has seventy-four members representing local districts. The President of the Nation is elected by all the voters for a term of four years.

Since the 1960s the Navajos have taken greater control of legal, educational, and health services in their Nation. The Tribal Council actively supports the Nation's rights to govern itself. This idea of self-government, or sovereignty, is guaranteed by treaties between native peoples and the United States.

LAND CLAIMS ▪ One issue that concerns every government is the boundaries of its territory. The Navajos are currently involved in negotiations over land with the neighboring Hopis. The disagreement between them involves an area of land used by both groups. When the Hopi Reservation was established in

1882, a presidential order stated that it was intended for use by "Hopis and other Indians." Since the Navajo population was increasing, and since American ranchers and farmers were intruding on Navajo territory, some Navajos moved onto the Hopi Reservation. At first, the two groups lived in harmony, but problems later arose because they both needed more land.

In the 1950s the Navajos and Hopis held meetings to try to settle the dispute over land. A panel of three federal judges then decided to give the Hopis ownership of land where their villages were located. The remaining land was named a joint-use area. Both Navajos and Hopis were allowed to live within this area, consisting of nearly 2 million acres (809,400 hectares). The judges' decision, however, did not solve the problem because it did not state where each group could live, farm, and graze their animals.

In an attempt to settle the issue, the United States Congress passed the Navajo-Hopi Settlement Act in 1974. The act officially divided the land in the joint-use area evenly between the two groups. People living on land given to the other group had to move within a period of five years. Two to three thousand Navajo families were affected. Many people resisted the move because they did not want to abandon their farms and grazing lands. Faced with strong opposition, the federal government allowed more time and gave increased financial aid to help people who had to move. This issue is still not resolved to the satisfaction of the Navajo and Hopi people.

EDUCATION ▪ The Navajos have taken steps to manage their own educational programs. In 1966 they started the first community-controlled school at Rough Rock, Arizona. Since

*By the 1970s the Navajos had taken over more
of their own educational programs, although supplies
and teaching materials remained scarce.*

then, several similar schools have opened. The schools have
bilingual and bicultural programs. Children in the early grades
are taught in the Navajo language and learn English later as a
second language. Community schools encourage parents and
local residents to participate in educational programs. They
invite traditional healers, spiritual leaders, and artisans to
teach children about their cultural and religious heritage.

The Navajos have also promoted higher education for their people. The Navajo Community College opened in 1969 at Tsaile, Arizona. A second branch was later started at Shiprock, New Mexico. The Tribal Council provides scholarships for students attending colleges both in the Navajo Nation and elsewhere in the United States. In 1973, the Navajos organized a Teacher Education Development Program to train Navajos who want to become elementary and secondary school teachers. The program operates through several universities in Arizona and New Mexico.

HEALTH CARE ▪ The Navajos are greatly concerned about health care services available in the Navajo Nation. The health status of the Navajo people is generally far below United States averages. They suffer from diseases such as pneumonia, influenza, and tuberculosis at high rates. Infant mortality rates are also higher than among other Americans. One reason for the spread of infection is that there are no running water, heating, or sewer systems in remote parts of the Nation. Another reason is that there are extremely limited medical services.

The United States Division of Indian Health operates a number of hospitals and clinics in the Navajo Nation. However, these facilities do not have enough doctors and nurses to treat all the people who need health care. Because of the poor care that the Navajos sometimes receive at hospitals and clinics, many people do not go to doctors when they are sick. They prefer to get treatment from traditional chanters.

In order to improve medical services, the Tribal Council and the Indian Health Service encourage cooperation between

Navajo chanters and American doctors. Native healers are asked to send their patients to hospitals for illnesses that they cannot treat. And American doctors are trained to respect traditional medicine and recognize its advantages in treating some diseases. In 1972 a Navajo Health Authority was established to promote both standard and traditional medical treatment. The authority has programs to educate people about the importance of sanitation and preventive health care.

WORK AND INCOME ▪ Economic development remains a serious problem for the Navajos. Although some people still engage in traditional activities such as farming, herding, and weaving, most Navajos are developing new sources of income. Navajo farmers and sheepherders face difficulties because much of the land is of poor quality. About one fifth of the Nation's land cannot be used for farming or grazing. Nearly half the remaining territory is of poor or only fair quality.

In order to generate income, the Tribal Council sponsors a number of businesses to sell goods produced in the Navajo Nation. The council funds forest industries, utilities, and housing projects. And the Arts and Crafts Guild sells jewelry, rugs, and paintings made by Navajo artists.

Some of the Navajo Nation's natural resources are mined by American companies. The Nation receives money from leases given to companies that mine the rich deposits of oil, gas, coal, and uranium. Although the Navajos earn money from these resources, some people oppose this use of their land because of the methods employed and the dangers to land and health. Coal companies use a technique called strip-mining

A roadside stand with silver and turquoise jewelry and handwoven rugs for sale near the Grand Canyon. The Navajos depend on profits from these and other businesses.

that removes coal near the surface and leaves the land barren and unsuitable for farming or grazing. Uranium is a radioactive mineral that severely threatens the lives of miners and nearby residents. Indeed, medical studies report high rates of cancer among Navajo uranium miners and their families. Studies found that some workers lived in houses built with radioactive materials. In addition, many Navajos object to the mining companies because mines often damage areas of land that the people consider sacred.

The Navajos seek jobs on or near the Nation to support themselves and their families. A majority of workers are employed in public services, including offices of the Navajo Nation, the federal Bureau of Indian Affairs, schools, and public health facilities. Some Navajos own local stores and businesses, while others work as teachers, nurses, doctors, and engineers.

■ ■ ■

The Navajos today successfully combine new ways of living with their valued traditions. They attend schools and colleges and also learn from their parents and grandparents. They speak Navajo and English. When they are sick, they seek the aid of both doctors and traditional chanters. They are farmers, herders, educators, office workers, and scientists. And when Navajos look around their land, they may think of the Holy People who protect them, remembering the words of an ancient prayer:

In beauty may we dwell.
In beauty may we walk.
In beauty may it rain on us.
In beauty may our corn grow.
In beauty all around us may it rain.
In beauty may we walk.
The beauty is restored.

A NAVAJO STORY:
THE CREATION OF FIRST
MAN AND FIRST WOMAN

Late in the autumn they heard the distant sound of a great voice calling from the east. They listened and waited, and soon heard the voice nearer and louder than before. Once more they listened and heard it louder still, very near. A moment later four mysterious beings appeared. These were White Body, Blue Body, Yellow Body, and Black Body.

The gods told the people that they would come back in twelve days. On the morning of the twelfth day the people washed themselves well. Then the women dried their skin with yellow cornmeal, the men with white cornmeal. Soon they heard the distant call, shouted four times, of the approaching gods. When the gods appeared, Blue Body and Black Body each carried a sacred buckskin. White Body carried two ears of corn, one yellow and one white.

The gods laid one buckskin on the ground with the head to the west, and on this they placed the two ears of corn with their tips to the east. Over the corn they spread the other buckskin with its head to the east. Under the white ear they put the feather of a white eagle; under the yellow ear the feather of a yellow eagle. Then they told the people to stand back and allow the wind to enter. Between the skins the white wind blew from the east and the yellow wind from the west. While the wind was blowing, eight gods called the Mirage People came and walked around the objects on the ground four times. As they walked, the eagle feathers, whose tips stuck out from the buckskins, were seen to move. When the Mirage People finished their walk, the upper buckskin was lifted. The ears of corn had disappeared; a man and a woman lay in their place.

The white ear of corn had become the man, the yellow ear had become the woman: First Man and First Woman. It was the wind that gave them life, and it is the wind that comes out of our mouths now that gives us life. When this ceases to blow, we die.

IMPORTANT DATES

1582	First contact between the Navajos and the Spanish, reported by Antonio de Espejo.
1680	The "Pueblo Revolt." The Navajos aid Puebloans by raiding Spanish soldiers.
1692–1696	Spanish reconquest of Puebloans in New Mexico and Arizona. The Navajos take in Tewa and Hopi refugees.
c. 1754	The Navajos leave Dinetah, move toward south and west into western New Mexico and eastern Arizona.
1849	Murder of Navajo leader Narbona and six aides as they leave a meeting with United States military officials.
1858	Bonneville Treaty between the Navajos and the United States. The Navajos agree to a reduction in the size of their territory.
1861	Treaty between the Navajos and the United States. Both groups pledge peace and friendship.
1863	Colonel Christopher (Kit) Carson begins military campaign to capture Navajos and force them to walk to Fort Sumner in eastern New Mexico (the Long Walk).
1864–1868	Imprisonment of the Navajos at Fort Sumner.

1868	Treaty signed between the Navajos and the United States when the Navajos are released from Fort Sumner. The Navajos return to a reservation of approximately 3.5 million acres (1.4 million hectares) only one-tenth the size of their original territory.
1921	Discovery of oil on the Navajo Reservation.
1923	Establishment of Navajo Tribal Council, consisting of twelve members appointed by the United States government.
1933	Beginning of stock reduction program aimed at decreasing the number of sheep owned by the Navajos.
1950	Navajo-Hopi Rehabilitation Act passed by United States Congress. The act provides almost $90 million for construction of wells, roads, schools, and health clinics.
1966	Founding of the first Navajo community-controlled bilingual school at Rough Rock, Arizona.
1969	Founding of the Navajo Community College at Tsaile, Arizona.
1974	Navajo-Hopi Settlement Act passed by United States Congress. The act divides the joint-use area of nearly 2 million acres (809,400 hectares) equally between the Navajos and the Hopis. Two to three thousand Navajo families living on the Hopis' portion are given five years to relocate.
1981	Navajo Nation opens an office in Washington, D.C., to lobby on behalf of the Navajos and to monitor federal policies and legislation affecting Native Americans.

GLOSSARY

Athapaskan. Language family that includes the Navajo language.

Clan. A group of people who believe that they are all descendants of a common ancestor.

Culture. The way of life followed by a group of people, including their work, family structure, social rules, political system, and religious beliefs.

Diagnostician. A person who specializes in finding out the cause of an illness.

Diné. The Navajos' name for themselves in their own language. *Diné* means "the people."

Dinetah. The original homeland of the Navajos in the Southwest. Dinetah was located in northwestern New Mexico and northeastern Arizona, south of the San Juan River.

Grazing districts. Land divisions in the Navajo Nation, each having a limit on the number of sheep allowed.

Hogan. A Navajo house built with six or eight sides. The door of a hogan always faces toward the east.

The Long Walk. The forced march of Navajos from their lands in Arizona to Fort Sumner in eastern New Mexico in 1864.

Navajo-Hopi Rehabilitation Act (1950). An act of the United States Congress that gave a sum of almost $90 million to the Navajos and Hopis for construction of wells, roads, schools, and clinics.

Navajo-Hopi Settlement Act (1974). An act of the United States Congress that divided the Navajo-Hopi joint-use area into two equal regions. One region was given to the Navajos, the other to the Hopis.

Pueblo Revolt. An uprising of Puebloan Indians in the Southwest against the Spanish. The revolt took place in 1680.

Reservation. An area of land owned by a group of Native American people.

Sandpainting (also called drypainting). A painting, made with colored sand, that is used in healing rituals.

Singer. A Navajo healer and ceremonial leader.

Sovereignty. The right of a people to self-government and control over their own nation.

Stock Reduction Program. A program ordered by the United States government to force Navajos to sell off a large percentage of their sheep. Stock reduction took place in the 1930s and 1940s.

Treaty. A legal agreement signed between two nations.

Tribal Council. The legal body of government on a reservation. The Navajo Tribal Council has seventy-four members who are elected by people in local districts.

BIBLIOGRAPHY

*Books for children

Bailey, Garrick, and Roberta Bailey. *A History of the Navajo: The Reservation Years.* Santa Fe: School of American Research Press, 1986.

Downs, James. *The Navajo.* New York: Holt, Rinehart & Winston, 1969.

Dyk, Walter (ed.). *Son of Old Man Hat: A Navajo Autobiography.* Lincoln: University of Nebraska Press, 1938 and 1967.

Dyk, Walter, and Ruth Dyk (eds.). *Left-Handed: A Navajo Autobiography.* New York: Columbia University Press, 1980.

Forbes, Jack. *Apache, Navaho, and Spaniard.* Norman: University of Oklahoma Press, 1960.

Hoffman, Virginia, and Broderick Johnson. *Navajo Biographies.* Rough Rock, AZ: Navajo Curriculum Center, Rough Rock Demonstration School, 1970.

*Kreischer, Elsie. *Navajo Magic of Hunting.* Billings, MT: Council for Indian Education, 1988.

Lamphere, Louise. *To Run After Them: Cultural and Social Bases of Cooperation in a Navajo Community.* Tuscon: University of Arizona Press, 1977.

Ortiz, A. (ed.) *Handbook of North American Indians.* Vol. 10. Washington, D.C.: Smithsonian Institution Press, 1983.

*Roessel, Monty. *Kinaalda: A Navajo Girl Grows Up.* Minneapolis: Lerner Publications, 1993.

Roessel, Ruth (ed.). *Navajo Stories of the Long Walk Period.* Tsaile, Navajo Nation: Navajo Community College Press, 1973.

*Sneve, Virginia Driving Hawk. *The Navajos: A First Americans Book.* New York: Holiday House, 1993.

*Stan, S. *The Navajo.* Vero Beach, FL.: Rourke Corp., 1989.

U.S. Commission on Civil Rights. *The Navajo Nation: An American Colony.* Washington, D.C., 1975.

U.S. Federal Trade Commission. *The Trading Post System on the Navajo Reservation.* Washington, D.C., 1973.

*Wood, Leigh H. *The Navajos.* New York: Chelsea House, 1993.

INDEX

Page numbers in *italics* refer to illustrations.

Jewelry, 43, *53*

Long Walk, 10, 40

Masks, *31*
Mexican-American War, 9, 38, *39*
Mining, 52–53
Mount Taylor, 26

Narbona, 12
Natural resources, 44–46, 52–53
Navajo-Hopi Rehabilitation Act of
    1950, 46–47
Navajo-Hopi Settlement Act of
    1974, 49
Navajo Indians
    ancestors of, 14–16
    children, 23, 25, 43, 44, 47, *50*
    community life of, 17–18, 20,
        22–23, 25
    crafts and, 20, *42*, 43, *53*
    education and, 43, *44*, 47, 49–
        51, *50*
    families, 17–18, 23, 25
    food of, 15, 21, 22, 28
    health care and, 51–52
    housing of, *15*, 18
    imprisonment of, *11*, 13–14, 40
    Long Walk and, 10, 40
    population of, 38, 42
    religion and, 26–28, *27*, 30–32,
        31, *33*, 34, 44
    settlers and, 12, 13, 16, 41–43
    Spanish and, 16, 35–37, *39*
    stock reduction program and,
        45–46
    territory of, 13, 14, 17, *22*, 41,
        43, 48–49

Tribal Council of, 45, 46, 48
U.S. government and, 9–13, 40,
    43–46, 49, 51
values of, 25
women, 18, 20, 25
Nofchissey, Arliene, 29

Oil, 44–46, 52

Prayersticks, *33*
Puebloans, 15, 16, 35–37
Pueblo Revolt, 36

Rainfall, 17, 22, 23
Religion, 26–28, *27*, 30–32, *31*,
    33, 34, 44

Sandpainting, 32, *33*, 34
San Francisco Mountain, 27
Sierra Blanca peak, 26–27
Slavery, 10, 13, 38
Stock reduction program, 45–46
Strip-mining, 52–53

Tewa Indians, 37
Tourists, 43
Treaty of 1868, 13
Tribal Council, 45, 46, 48, 51

United States government, 9–13,
    40, 43–46, 49, 51
Uranium, 52, 53
Ute Indians, 10, 37

Values, 25

Weaving, 20, *42*, 43, 52
Women, 18, 20, 25